P9-DNQ-093

ER 591.77 BRE
Bredeson, Carmen.
Leafy sea dragons and other
weird sea creatures / Carmen
Bredeson.

I LIKE WEIRD ANIMALS!

Leafy Sea Dragons and Other Weird Sea Creatures

FOUNTAINDALE PUBLIC LIBRARY DISTRICT
300 West Briarcliff Road
Bolingbrook, IL 60440-2894
(630) 759-2102

Series Science Consultant:
Dennis L. Claussen, PhD
Professor of Zoology
Miami University
Oxford, OH

Series Literacy Consultant:
Allan A. De Fina, PhD
Dean, College of Education/Professor of Literacy Education
New Jersey City University
Past President of the New Jersey Reading Association

Carmen Bredeson

CONTENTS

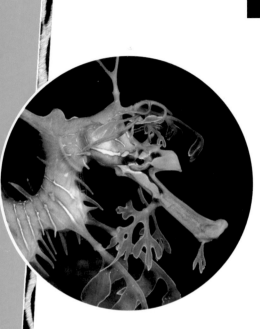

WORDS TO KNOW

anemone (uh NEH muh nee)—A type of ocean animal that looks like a plant.

enemy (EH nuh mee)—An animal that tries to kill or is a threat to another animal.

parasite (PAR uh syt)—A tiny animal that lives in or on another animal.

wrasse (RASS)—A type of fish that cleans another fish's mouth.

Sea Creatures

Seas cover much of the earth.

There are many kinds of animals that live in the sea.

Some of them look strange.

Others do strange things.

Which sea animal is your favorite?

A lionfish uses its long spines to sting its enemies.

ANGLERFISH

An anglerfish has a strange part growing out of its head.

It looks like a fishing rod.

The end of the rod lights up.

Other fish swim toward the light to see what it is.

Gulp! The anglerfish just caught its lunch.

CLEANER WRASSE

A big fish opens its mouth wide.

Little **wrasses** swim right into the huge mouth.

They clean bits of food and **parasites** from the teeth, mouth, and gills.

The big fish does not try to eat the cleaner wrasses.

PORCUPINE FISH

When an **enemy** is near, a porcupine fish GULPS water.

Its body blows up like a balloon.

The porcupine fish has scales that are sharp and pointed.

When the fish blows up, the scales stick straight out.

Who would want to eat that?

HERMIT CRAB

A hermit crab uses its claws to pick up a sea **anemone**.

The crab puts the anemone on top of its shell.

Sea anemones are stinging animals that look like plants.

The anemones help scare away the crab's enemies.

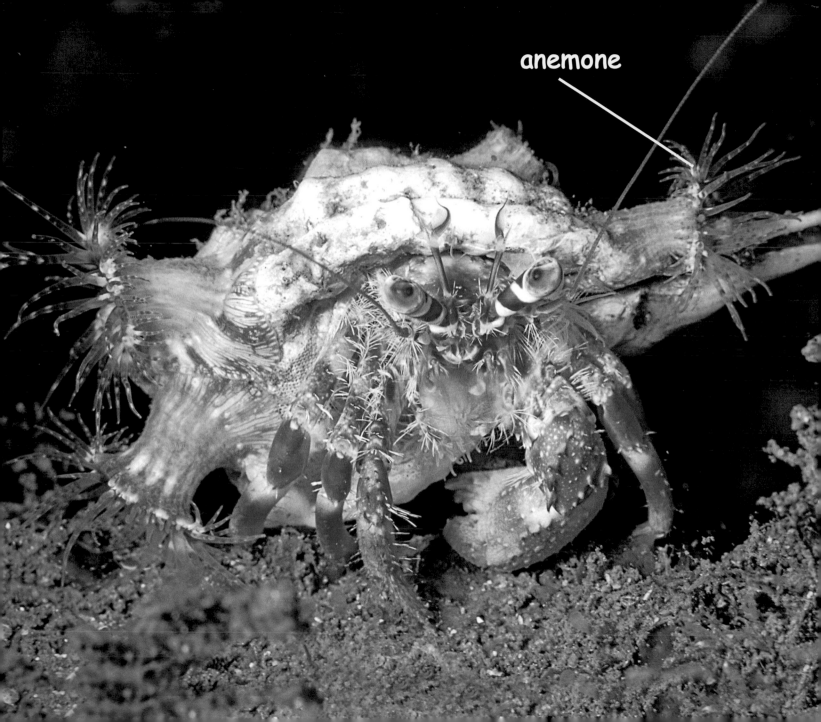

anemone

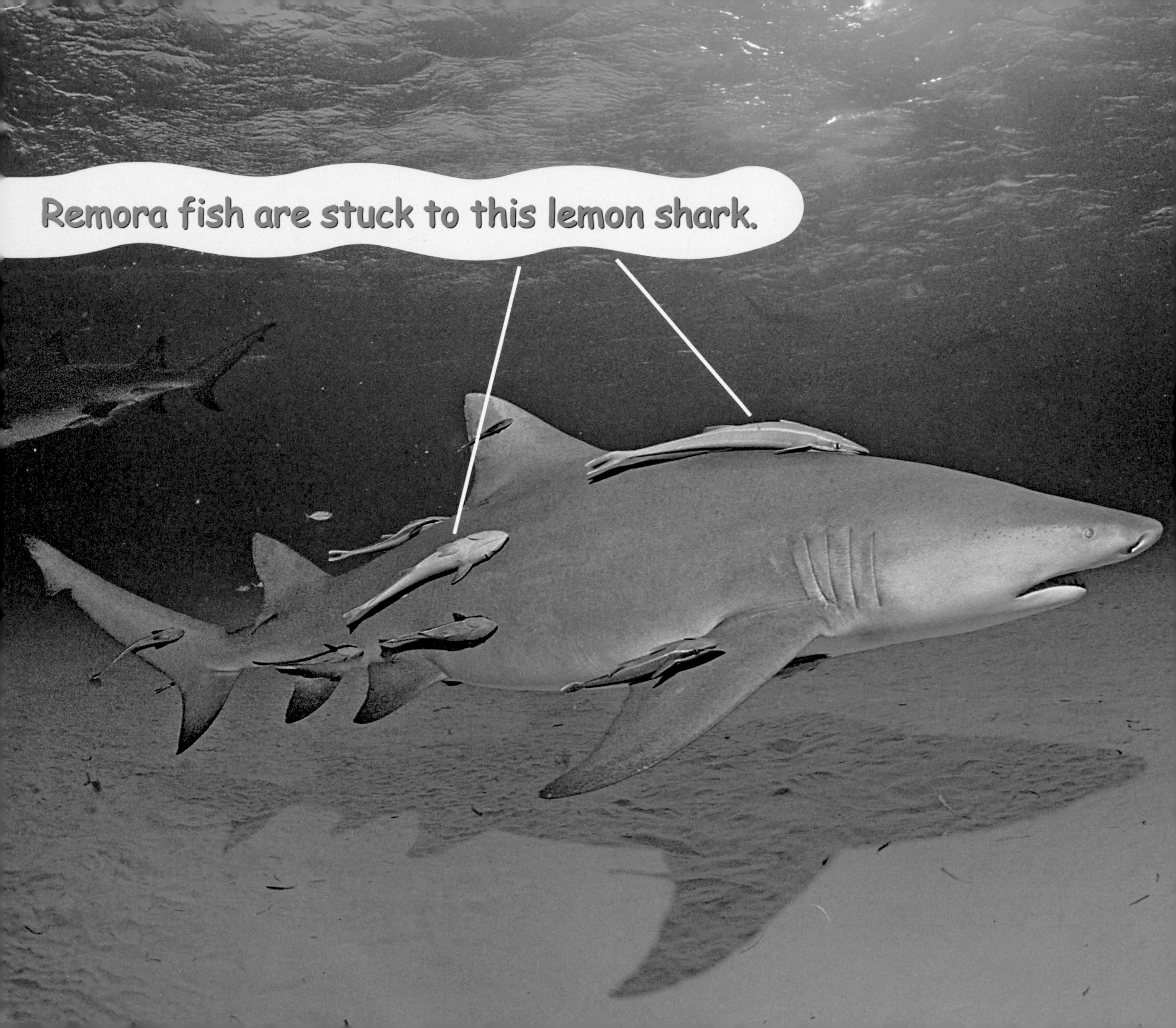
Remora fish are stuck to this lemon shark.

REMORA FISH

The little remora (re MOR uh) fish has a sucker on the top of its head.

It sticks itself onto a bigger fish.

The remora gets a free ride.

It also gets the scraps of food left over after the bigger fish eats.

LEAFY SEA DRAGON

Leafy sea dragons look like seaweed.

They have frilly parts all over their bodies.

Hiding from enemies is easy for them.

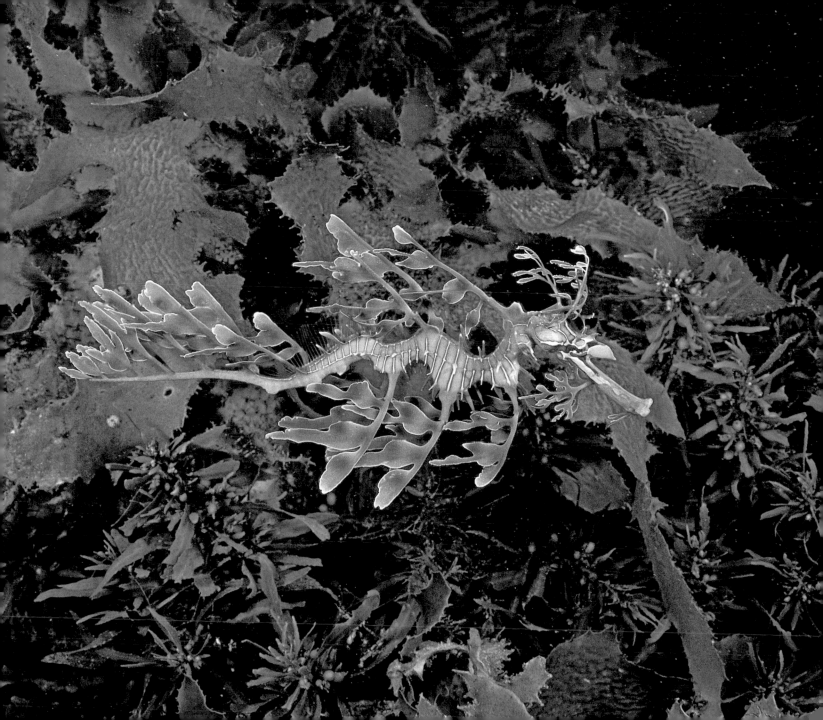

yellowtail flounder

FLOUNDER

A young flounder has an eye on each side of its head.

Then the fish grows. One of its eyes moves to the other side of its head.

Now it has two eyes on one side.

When the flounder lies flat on the ocean bottom, it can see with both eyes.

peacock flounder

OCEAN SUNFISH

Ocean sunfish can weigh as much as a small CAR.

The huge, round sunfish eat jellyfish, squid, and small fish.

Ocean sunfish do not mind when divers swim around them.

LEARN MORE

Books

Gross, Miriam. *The Sea Dragon*. New York: Powerkids Press, 2006.

McCall, Gerrie. *Weird & Wonderful Fish*. Strongsville, Ohio: Gareth Stevens Publishing, 2005.

Pohl, Kathleen. *Animals of the Ocean*. Strongsville, Ohio: Gareth Stevens Publishing, 2007.

LEARN MORE

Web Sites

National Geographic Creature Feature
<http://kids.nationalgeographic.com/Animals/CreatureFeature/>
Click on "Ocean."
See videos and pictures of your favorite sea animals.

NOAA
<http://school.discovery.com/schooladventures/planetocean/>
Download activity and coloring books.

Planet Ocean
<http://school.discovery.com/schooladventures/planetocean/>
Find photos and fun facts.

INDEX

For my weird siblings: Ralph, Jack, and Renee

Enslow Elementary, an imprint of Enslow Publishers, Inc.
Enslow Elementary® is a registered trademark of Enslow Publishers, Inc.

Copyright © 2010 by Carmen Bredeson

All rights reserved.

No part of this book may be reproduced by any means without the written permission of the publisher.

Library of Congress Cataloging-in-Publication Data

Bredeson, Carmen.
  Leafy sea dragons and other weird sea creatures / Carmen Bredeson.
    p. cm.—(I like weird animals!)
  Includes bibliographical references and index.
  Summary: "Provides young readers with facts about several strange sea creatures"—Provided by publisher.
  ISBN-13: 978-0-7660-3125-8
  ISBN-10: 0-7660-3125-X
  1. Marine animals—Miscellanea—Juvenile literature. I. Title.
  QL122.2.B743 2009
  591.77—dc22
                    2008021491

Printed in the United States of America

10 9 8 7 6 5 4 3 2 1

♻ Enslow Publishers, Inc., is committed to printing our books on recycled paper. The paper in every book contains 10% to 30% post-consumer waste (PCW). The cover board on the outside of each book contains 100% PCW. Our goal is to do our part to help young people and the environment too!

To Our Readers: We have done our best to make sure all Internet addresses in this book were active and appropriate when we went to press. However, the author and the publisher have no control over and assume no liability for the material available on those Internet sites or on other Web sites they may link to. Any comments or suggestions can be sent by e-mail to comments@enslow.com or to the address on the back cover.

Every effort has been made to locate all copyright holders of material used in this book. If any errors or omissions have occurred, corrections will be made in future editions of this book.

Photo Credits: © Fred Bavendam/Minden Pictures, pp. 1, 2; © Joyce & Frank Burek/Animals Animals, p. 19; © K. Gowlett-Holmes/OSF/Animals Animals, p. 10; © Minden Pictures/Getty Images, pp. 6, 15, 17; © Reinhard Dirscherl/Visuals Unlimited, pp. 5, 14; © Richard Herrmann/OSF/Animals Animals, p. 20; © Richard Herrmann/Visuals Unlimited, p. 21; © SeaPics.com, pp. 9, 13; © Stone/Getty Images, p. 18.

Cover Photo: © Fred Bavendam/Minden Pictures

Note to Parents and Teachers: The *I Like Weird Animals!* series supports the National Science Education Standards for K–4 science. The Words to Know section introduces subject-specific vocabulary words, including pronunciation and definitions. Early readers may need help with these new words.

Enslow Elementary
an imprint of
Enslow Publishers, Inc.
40 Industrial Road
Box 398
Berkeley Heights, NJ 07922
USA
http://www.enslow.com